Beside the Seaside

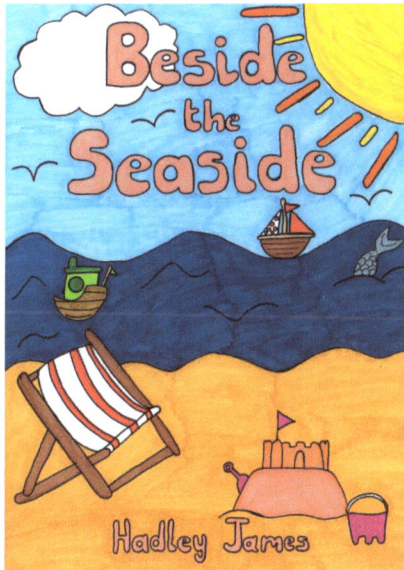

Hadley James

Contents

The Beach

Stripey towel,
In the sun,
Castles built,
Lots of fun.
Moat dug,
Shells found,
Happy People,
All around.

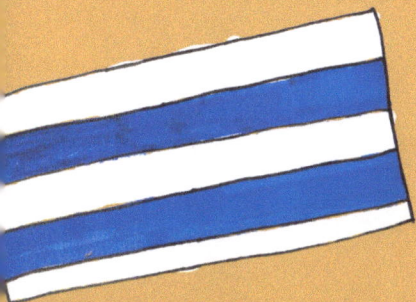

Tea for Two

Fish and chips,
By the sea,
A perfect treat,
Just for me.

Then I spy,
Watching me,
A seagull looking,
At my tea.

Don't you dare,
This is mine,
Hot and salty,
It's divine.

Seagull swoops,
Steals a chip,
Fly's away,
Gives me the slip!

Paddling

I love to paddle in the sea,
And watch the waves as they chase me.

I splish and splash and run and jump,
The waves hit me with a gentle bump.

I squidge the sand between my toes,
And watch the water as it flows.

The tide comes forward then creeps back.
The waves come for their next attack.

I love to paddle in the sea,
And watch the waves as they chase me!

Sandcastle Building

We rush down to the beach,
With bucket and spade in hand,
I'm going to build a palace,
The finest in the land.

I pile the sand in my bucket,
And fill it up to the brim,
Then flatten and pat down the top,
While my sister goes off for a swim.

My first castle is ready,
But that is just the start,
When I've built my whole kingdom,
It'll be a work of art.

I've placed four corner castles,
And next I build a wall,
And then right in the middle,
I build a keep so tall.

My palace is completed,
So now it's time to dig,
I make a moat around it,
It's wide and rather big.

From the moat I dig,
A channel to the sea,
And when it fills with water,
My face lights up with glee.

We decorate with shells,
And put a flag on the tower,
Then step back to admire it,
It only took an hour!

Now the kingdom is complete,
There's only one thing left,
We jump and smash the castle,
But now I feel bereft.

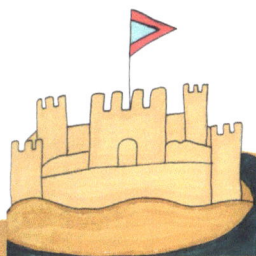

The Deep Sea

The deep blue sea,
Spoke to me,
It helped me to feel,
Wild and free.

I watched the waves,
That come and go,
Just like life's,
Sweet ebb and flow.

On the surface,
Ripples grow,
But all is calm,
Deep down below.

Candyfloss

Delicious
  Fluffy
    Sugar spun
      Bright pink
        On a stick
          Lots of fun
            Sticky
              Gooey
                Now a ball
                  Not sure
                    I can
                      Eat it all!

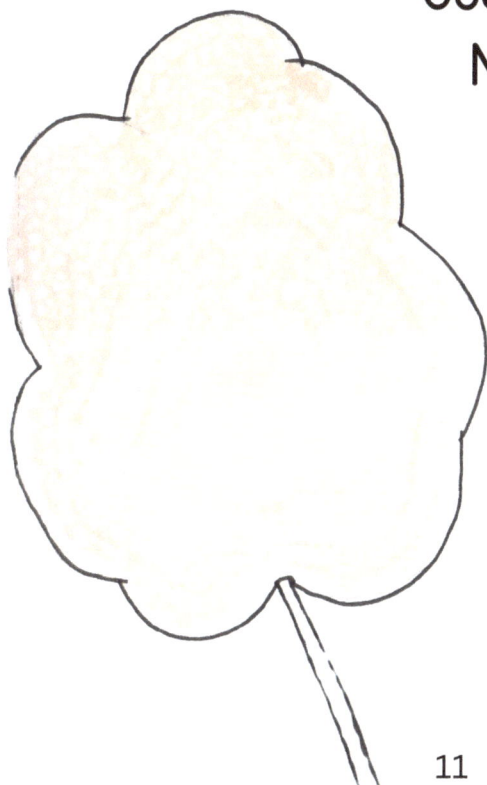

Seagulls

Surfing the waves,
Bobbing along,
Swept about,
On the tide so strong.

Watching the boats,
With beady eyes,
Looking for fish,
To steal as a prize.

In the air now,
Ready to swoop,
Spots the caught fish,
All in a big group.

No time to waste,
Have to be bold,
Grabs a huge fish,
To a seagull it's gold!

Shells

Like tiny treasures from the ocean,
I love to find shells on the beach,
Left behind by mermaids or monsters,
Waiting for me within my reach.

Their colours sparkle in the sun,
Like jewels from an unknown land,
Hard and smooth yet fragile too,
I love to hold them in my hand.

Rainy Day

Pitter patter, pitter patter,
Down falls the rain,
Pitter patter, pitter patter,
Here it comes again.

Pitter patter, pitter patter,
We are on the beach,
Pitter patter, pitter patter,
The sun is out of reach.

Pitter patter, pitter patter,
All over the sand,
Pitter patter, pitter patter,
It's getting out of hand.

Pitter patter, pitter patter,
Pack our things away,
Pitter patter, pitter patter,
The rain is here to stay.

Pitter patter, pitter patter,
We're back at the hotel,
Pitter patter, pitter patter,
We're soaking wet as well.

Pitter patter, pitter patter,
We're drying out inside,
Pitter patter, pitter patter,
The rain has made us hide.

The Harbour

The boats all line up at the harbour,
They bob up and down on the sea,
All sat moored in a line,
Just like they are waiting for me.

I long to be out on the ocean,
To feel the warm sun on my skin,
The cool sea would calm and soothe me,
And if I got hot I'd jump in.

But we are just sat in the harbour,
Watching the boats come and go,
One day I'll be out on the water,
But when that will be I don't know.

Rock

Stripey and colourful,
Sticky and sweet,
Crunchy and hard,
But so good to eat.

A delight to the eyes,
With flavours galore,
We've chosen three sticks,
But I always want more!

Jellyfish

Floating cloud,
Tentacles trailing,
Gliding gracefully,
Smooth sailing.

Beautiful creature,
But beware one thing,
Those tentacles,
Can really sting!

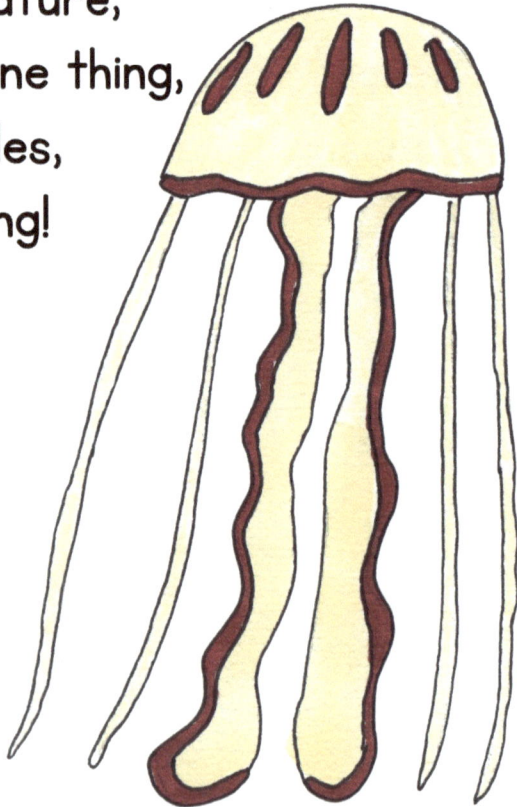

Rockpool Acrostic

R olling

O cean tides

C reate

K ingdoms

P ulsating

O verflowing with an

O asis of

L ife.

Catch a Wave

I'd love to catch a wave,
And hold it in my hand,
But they all run away,
And tease me on the sand.

They keep on coming back,
They knock me off my feet,
But when I can swim with them,
The feeling can't be beat.

I'd love to catch a wave,
But they want to be free,
They keep on dancing forwards,
Then retreat back to the sea.

Sand

Sand on the ground,
Sand in your toes,
Sand in your hand,
Sand up your nose.

Sand in your sandwiches,
Sand in your drink,
Sand in your eyes,
Making you blink.

Sand on your clothes,
Sand in your hair,
Sand in your bag,
It gets everywhere!

Ice Cream

One scoop,
Two scoops,
Three scoops,
Four.

Five scoops,
Six scoops,
Seven scoops,
More!

So many flavours to try,
I can see,
One scoop for you,
And two for me.

Vanilla, strawberry,
Chocolate too,
Toffee and mint,
And something that's blue.

In a cone or tub,
And covered of course,
With sprinkles, a flake,
And strawberry sauce!

The Sea

The sea is wild,
The sea is free,
The sea has depth,
And mystery.

The sea is blue,
The sea is deep,
The sea has secrets,
That it keeps.

The sea is brave,
The sea is bold,
The sea keeps treasures,
Of jewels and gold.

The sea is stormy,
The sea is rough,
The sea is fierce,
Taming it can be tough.

The sea is gentle,
The sea is calm,
The sea soothes me,
With its effortless charm.

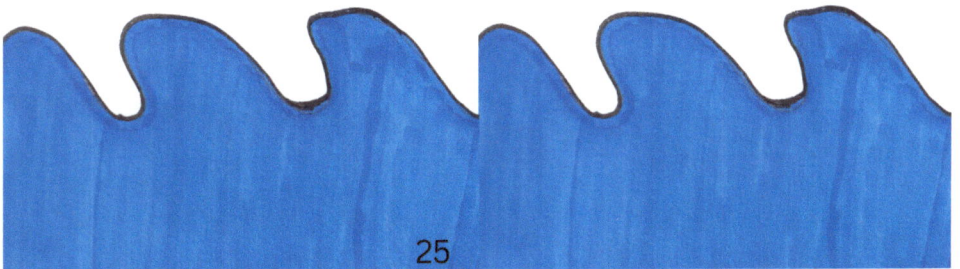

Bucket and Spade

Red, yellow,
Orange, green,
So many buckets,
I have seen!

Fill them with water,
Or fill them with sand,
Use them to build,
A castle so grand.

Fill up your bucket,
And dig with your spade,
Then just sit back,
And admire what you've made!

Arcades

Lots of games,
For us to play,
It's going to be,
A brilliant day!

Racing bikes,
Dancing to songs,
The music makes me,
Sing along.

My favourite game,
Is the 2p machine,
I put in one,
And get sixteen.

The claw machine,
Gives me a surprise,
The claw swoops down,
And I win a prize!

Boat Trip

We're going on a boat trip,
We're going out to sea,
We're going to look for seals,
And to see what we can see!

The sea is rough and choppy,
We bump upon the waves,
We go around the headland,
And past the smugglers' cave.

The seals are sunbathing,
They lay upon the rocks,
We take lots of photos,
Then head back to the docks.

The sea is calmer now,
It is a smoother ride,
We sail on peacefully,
Upon the rising tide.

Swimming in the Sea

It's hot on the sand,
But freezing in the sea,
I only dip my feet in,
Then go up to my knees.

It's far too cold,
It makes me want to scream,
But then I jump right in,
And it is like a dream.

I swim up and down,
Then try to surf the waves,
I swim up to the rocks,
And look around the caves.

I love to watch the fish,
And follow where they go,
It is a secret world,
In the kingdom down below.

Mermaid

I'd like to be a mermaid,
And live under the sea,
I'd look after all the fish,
And they'd look after me.

I'd sunbathe on the rocks,
And sing about the sea,
I'd look so beautiful,
And swim so gracefully.

I'd like to be a mermaid,
With a house under the sea,
I'd be friends with all the dolphins,
And invite them round for tea!

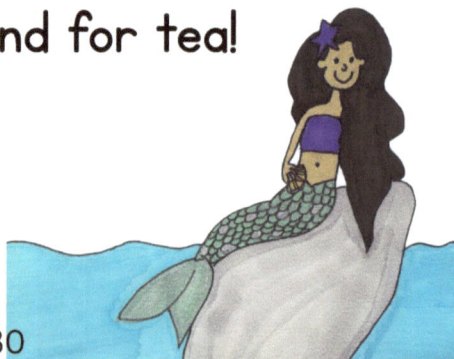

Donkey

I love to watch the donkeys,
As they plod along the sand,
So gentle and so friendly,
They're always in demand.

They like to stay together,
And walk in a long line,
I think they're wonderful,
I wish that they were mine!

Catch of the Day

We're fishing from the pier,
It's a bright and sunny day,
I hope I catch something,
I hope a big fish comes my way.

The lines are very still,
Like nothing's going on,
We're waiting for a bite,
But it seems that there are none.

The person next to us,
Is reeling something in,
It seems very big,
But I think he's going to win.

Suddenly, a tug,
I think I've got a bite,
I try to reel it in,
And pull with all my might.

It must be a whooper,
It is such hard work,
Then suddenly the line goes slack,
And comes up with a jerk.

I can't wait to see my catch,
And celebrate my loot,
But I haven't caught a fish,
It's an old and smelly boot!

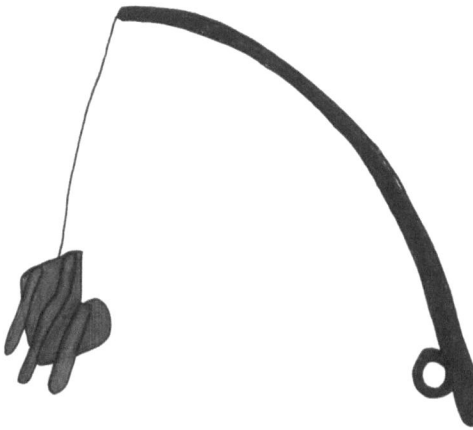

Fairground

The fairground is alive,
With music and with lights,
I love being here,
And seeing all the sights.

I think I'll hook a duck,
I hope I win a prize,
I did! I won! Hooray!
I chose a lucky dip surprise!

Next we're on the dodgems,
We drive around the track,
We're not very good at dodging,
And people bump into our back.

Now I'm feeling peckish,
So we stop to have a treat,
Delicious, fluffy candy floss,
So sticky and so sweet.

I really love the fairground,
There's so much to enjoy,
It's the perfect place to visit,
And you might even win a toy!

Also by Hadley James:

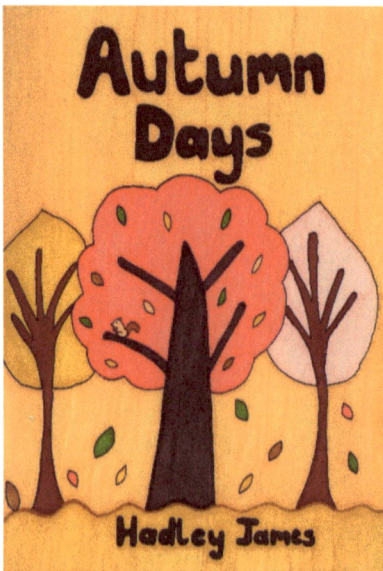

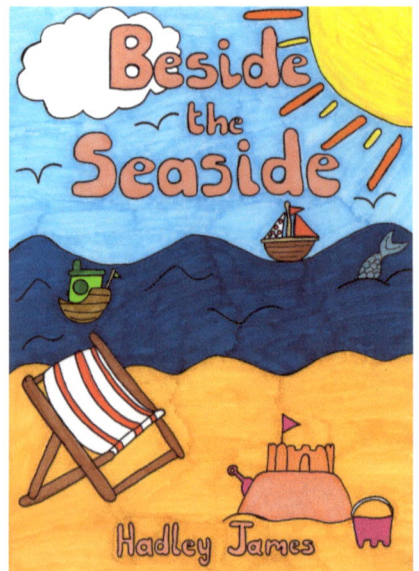

Wonderful
Me

Hadley James

Horrid
Halloween

Hadley James

Autumn
Days

Hadley James

Beside
the
Seaside

Hadley James

Wonderful Winter
Hadley James

Spectacular Spring
Hadley James

Grand Days Out
Zoo
Circus
Hadley James

Extreme Environments
Hadley James

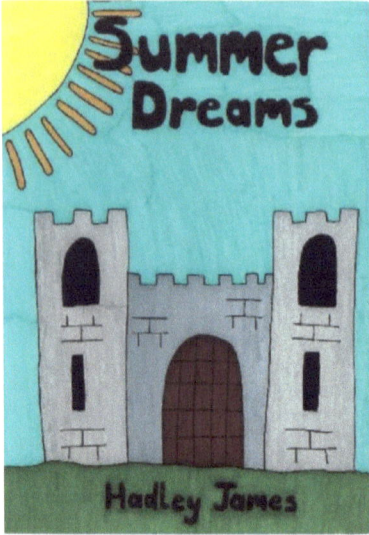

Summer Dreams

Hadley James

Marvellous Minibeasts

Hadley James

Fabulous Farm

Hadley James

www.ingramcontent.com/pod-product-compliance
Lightning Source LLC
Chambersburg PA
CBHW041803040426
42448CB00001B/26